THE POWER OF PRESSURE

ANDREW DUNN
Illustrated by
ED CARR

Thomson Learning

New York

Titles in this series

Heat
It's Electric
Lifting by Levers
The Power of Pressure
Simple Slopes
Wheels at Work

Library of Congress Cataloging-in-Publication Data
Dunn, Andrew.
    The power of pressure / Andrew Dunn ; illustrated by Ed Carr.
        p.   cm.—(How things work)
    Includes bibliographical references and index.
    Summary: Explains how air and water pressure work and how they are
used in machines.
    ISBN 1-56847-015-0
    1. Compressed air—Juvenile literature.   2. Water—Juvenile literature.
3. Hydraulic machinery—Juvenile literature. [1. Compressed air.
2. Water.   3. Hydraulic machinery.   4. Machinery.]   I. Carr, Ed, ill.
II. Title.   III. Series: Dunn, Andrew. How things work.
TJ985.D85   1993
621.5′1—dc20   92-41512

First published in the
United States in 1993 by
Thomson Learning
115 Fifth Avenue
New York, NY 10003

First published in 1992 by
Wayland (Publishers) Ltd
61 Western Road, Hove
East Sussex, BN3 1JD, England

Printed in the United States of America

Contents

Words in *italic* in the text are explained in the glossary on page 30.

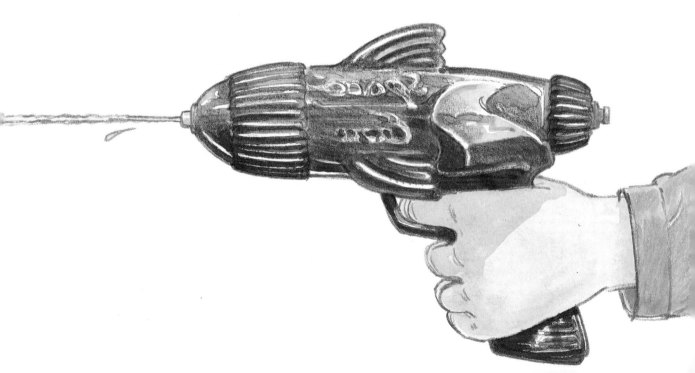

The force in fluids

Machines, whether as simple as a bottle opener or as complicated as a space rocket, all need effort, or force, to do their jobs. Some machines take this force from the power of human muscles or from electricity. But some machines use the pressure of fluids.

Pressure is all around us. It is any force pressing on a surface. A fluid is anything that can flow—a gas, such as air, or a liquid, such as water. All fluids push on the things around them with pressure.

The tiny *particles* of gases are moving all the time, bumping into each other and any surface they hit. The air around us has pressure because of this constant movement, and also because of the enormous weight of all the air above us.

In liquids, the particles do not move as much as in gases, so pressure is mostly caused by the liquid's own weight or by something trying to squash it.

This scene looks calm, but the tiny particles of the air and water are moving all the time.

How much pressure?

Air pressure is stronger than you might think. Try this experiment (over a sink, just in case!).

Fill a glass or cup to the brim with water. Cover it with a piece of cardboard. Now, holding the cardboard in place, turn the glass upside down. Let go of the cardboard. What happens?

Air pressure holds the water in. It presses up on the cardboard with far more force than the weight of the water pushing down.

Luckily the pressure of the fluids inside our bodies just about *balances* the air pressure outside, or we would be squashed flat!

Some pressure machines

Machines use pressure in many different ways. Some machines use liquids, such as oil or water. Others use gases, such as *carbon dioxide*. Most use air pressure. Some pressure machines blow or spray, and some use *suction*. Can you see which of these machines blow and which use suction?

Drinking straw

Hovercraft

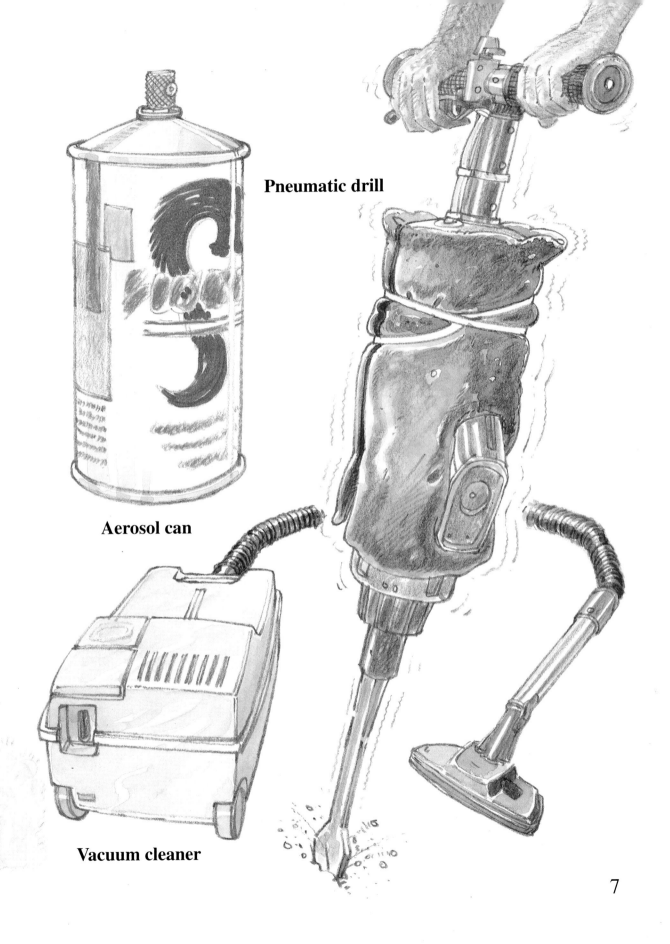

Pneumatic drill

Aerosol can

Vacuum cleaner

7

The principle of pressure

You can increase pressure in any fluid by squeezing—or *compressing*—lots of it into a small space. You can also lower its pressure by giving it more room. But nature likes things to balance each other. The principle of all pressure machines is this: any fluid will move, if it can, until it has the same pressure as its surroundings.

You can compress air into a balloon by blowing into it. But when you let go, air will rush out. It will keep coming out until the air inside has the same pressure as the air outside.

A balloon stays blown up if no air can escape. But when you let it go the extra air rushes out.

8

Strong pressure

Pressure can be a very strong force. Normally, because air is spread evenly all around us, and because our bodies are full of blood and water at about the same pressure as the air outside, we do not notice air pressure. You have only to take some air out of one place, though, or put some into another, and the balance will have gone. Then you will notice the effects of pressure.

Pressure pumps

A simple kind of pump is a *piston* in a *cylinder* of water with a small hole at one end. Moving the piston makes the "box" of water smaller or bigger.

When the "box" is made smaller, the water pressure goes up. The water will escape the only way it can—through the hole—in a powerful jet of water.

When the piston moves back to make the "box" bigger, air or water will be sucked in until the pressure inside balances the pressure outside.

Valves

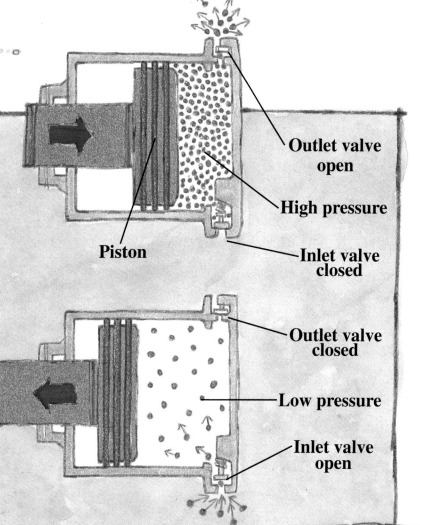

Some pumps use a clever system of *valves*.

When the piston is pushed into the cylinder, the pressure closes the inlet valve and opens the outlet valve so that the gas or liquid is forced out.

As the piston is pulled out again, the outlet valve shuts and the inlet valve opens. The fluid is sucked in from outside, then forced out through the outlet when the piston is pushed back in.

Outlet valve open

High pressure

Piston

Inlet valve closed

Outlet valve closed

Low pressure

Inlet valve open

Bicycle pumps use valves to push air into tires.

More pumps

The piston pump and bicycle pump both have a part—a piston—that moves back and forth to increase pressure on the fluid.

Other pumps, however, use a circular, or rotary, movement to increase pressure. These pumps work in different ways, but they are all useful in that they can produce a steady stream of pressurized fluid.

Rotary pumps are used in car engines and gasoline pumps.

Gas stations use rotary pumps. The gasoline is pulled up from big tanks underground.

Cooling system

Car engines need to be cooled by a steady flow of water. The water is pushed around the engine by a rotary pump.

The round pump contains *blades* that spin around. Water enters at the center of the pump and the revolving blades swirl it around, flinging it outward.

The water leaves through an outlet in the wall of the pump at high pressure.

It is pushed through the engine and becomes hot.

It then goes through the car's radiator where it is cooled, ready to be pumped around the engine again.

Pneumatic machines

Pneumatic machines use air pressure. The pneumatic tire, for example, simply contains air at high pressure, providing an air "cushion" between the wheel and the ground. This evens out the bumps and makes for a smoother journey.

Hovercraft

Skirt

Fan

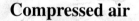

Compressed air

A hovercraft rides on a cushion of air.

Air is sucked in and compressed by big fans inside the hovercraft, giving it enough force to lift the craft and its passengers.

The air is held in under the hovercraft by a thick skirt made of rubber.

The hovercraft floats above the surface of the ground or sea without causing *friction*. Normal propellers push it along.

Pneumatic drill (or jackhammer)

① Compressed air enters drill

② Valve lets air into outer compartment

④ Piston rises and forces valve open

③ Air in inner compartment pushes up piston

⑤ Valve lets in compressed air

⑥ Piston is pushed down to hit drill

The jackhammer uses compressed air to force a piston up and down inside a shaft. The piston repeatedly thumps the heavy tool that batters the road surface, breaking it up with great force—and an ear-splitting noise!

Hydraulic machines

Car brakes

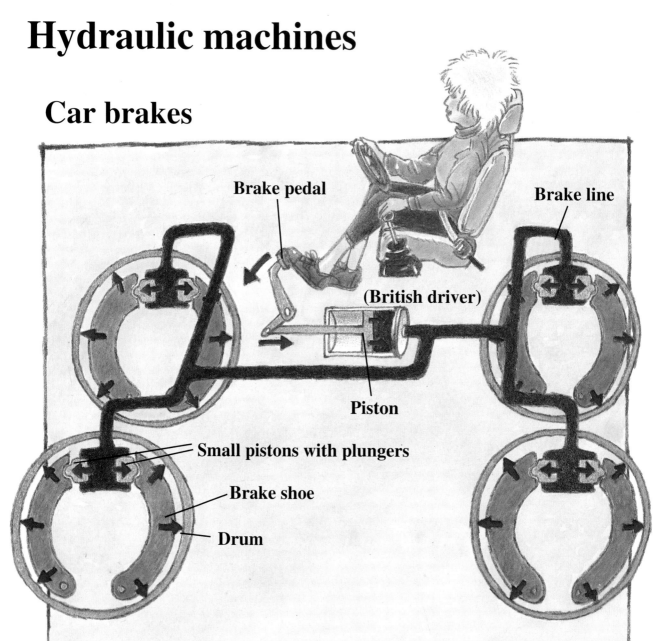

Brake pedal

Brake line

(British driver)

Piston

Small pistons with plungers

Brake shoe

Drum

Car brakes are *hydraulic* machines. *Hydraulic* means they work by the pressure in liquids.

The brake pedal pushes down a piston in a cylinder, which is connected by pipes, or "lines," to smaller cylinders, also with pistons, in the wheel drums.

The whole system is filled with oil. This oil does not compress much, so pushing on the main piston immediately affects the rest of the system.

The oil pushes the smaller pistons, and plungers push the brake shoes against the drums. This friction slows down the car.

Hydraulic lift

You can see another hydraulic machine lifting heavy cars in a garage. It has one piston, under the lift platform.

Compressed air is pumped into an oil tank, which is connected to a cylinder containing the piston.

The air forces the oil into the cylinder under strong pressure.

The pressure under the platform becomes greater than the weight of the car on top, and the piston rises. Closing the oil valve keeps the oil compressed and the platform raised.

Piston

Oil valve

Compressed air

Oil

Sprays and jets

When a liquid is forced through a small hole, it forms a powerful jet. This jet usually breaks up into a spray of tiny droplets in the air.

The *nozzle* of an *aerosol* spray can is so tiny that the spray becomes a fine mist. Many liquid products, such as hair sprays and bug killers, work better as a spray.

Dishwasher

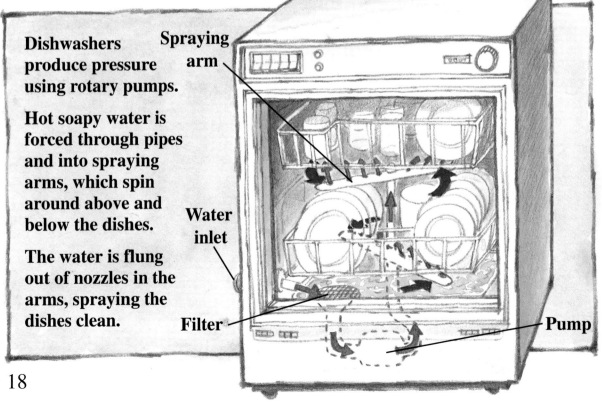

Dishwashers produce pressure using rotary pumps.

Hot soapy water is forced through pipes and into spraying arms, which spin around above and below the dishes.

The water is flung out of nozzles in the arms, spraying the dishes clean.

Spraying arm

Water inlet

Filter

Pump

Aerosol can

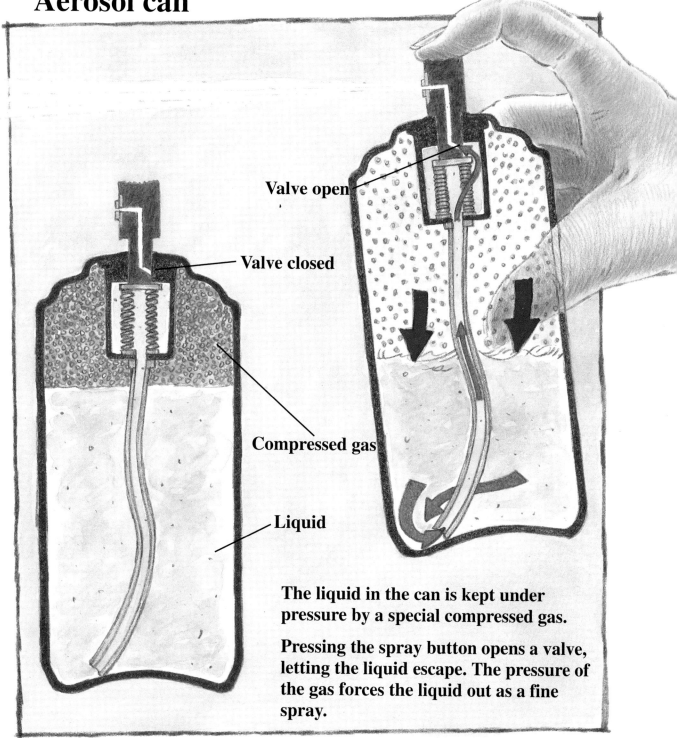

Valve open

Valve closed

Compressed gas

Liquid

The liquid in the can is kept under pressure by a special compressed gas.

Pressing the spray button opens a valve, letting the liquid escape. The pressure of the gas forces the liquid out as a fine spray.

Sucking machines

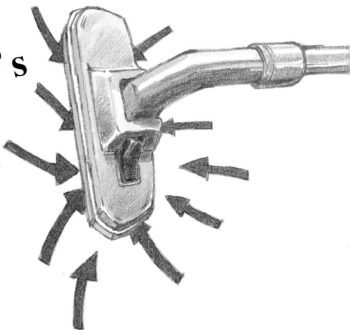

Most machines that work by pressure use compression to blow or force something outward. But the balance can also be upset the other way, by removing pressure. Removing pressure causes suction.

When you drink through a straw, you start by sucking the air out of it. This means that there is no air pressing down on the drink inside the straw.

But air is still pressing down on the drink in the cup, and that forces the drink up the straw, into your mouth.

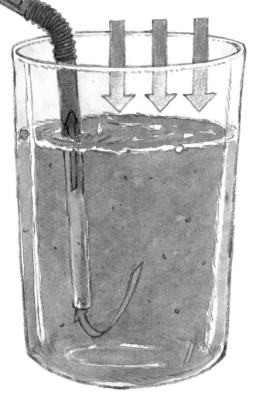

When you stop sucking, the air pressure at each end of the straw is equal. The milk slips down again.

Vacuum cleaner

The vacuum cleaner uses suction, too. An electric fan blows air out of the back of the cleaner, leaving low air pressure inside.

The outside air rushes in to fill the gap, bringing all the dust and dirt with it.

It passes through a filter, which stops the dust but not the air.

The dust is collected in a bag, but the air is pumped out again, so that more air is sucked in — and with it, more dust.

Filter bag

Fan

Electric motor

The siphon

In a siphon, pressure makes water flow uphill! You can make a siphon with a piece of plastic or clean rubber tubing. You can buy this from a model store.

Put one end of the tubing into a bowl of water and suck at the other end until the tube is full of water.

Put a finger over this end to hold the water in, and lower it into the sink.

As long as this end of the tube is lower than the other end, water will flow up from the bowl and down into the sink.

The weight of the water in the tube makes the siphon start flowing, and air pressure on the water in the bowl does the rest.

Air pressure

Toilet cistern

Some toilets flush using a siphon. A tube goes up from the *cistern* and down into the toilet bowl.

Ball cock

Disk

Valve

1 Disk raises water to start siphon.

When the handle is pushed down, it pulls up a disk, which takes water up with it and starts the siphon flowing. It only stops when the cistern is almost empty.

2 Weight of water in pipe keeps siphon flowing.

By then the floating *ball cock* has fallen far enough to open a valve, which allows the cistern to refill.

3 Cistern empties and siphon is broken. Lowered ball cock opens valve.

The siphon is now full of air, and nothing will happen until the handle is pressed down again.

4 Cistern refills and valve closes.

23

Experiments with pressure

Here are some pressure tricks
you can try on your friends!

The obedient shower

**Use a corkscrew to make
a few holes in the base of
an empty squeeze bottle.**

**Put the bottle in a bowl of
water and squeeze out all
the air. Then loosen your
grip.**

**Before you take the bottle
out of the water, place
your finger over the hole
in the nozzle at the top.**

**When you take the bottle
out and lift your finger,
the shower will start.
Cover the hole again and
it will stop.**

**The water can only fall
from the bottom when air
can press down on the
top. Otherwise, the air
outside, pushing up from
underneath, holds
the water in.**

The spouting fountain

CAUTION:
For safety,
have an adult
help you with
this experiment.

Take a glass screw-top bottle and half fill it with cool water. You could add a few drops of food coloring for fun.

Have an adult make a hole in the cap by hammering a nail into it. Screw the cap firmly on to the bottle.

Push a straw through the hole until it is well under the water, and *seal* it to the cap with modeling clay.

Plug the top of the straw with modeling clay as well, and make a hole in the clay with a pin.

Carefully fill a bucket with hot water, put the bottle into the bucket and hold it there. The water in the bottle will spurt out like a fountain.

The hot water heats the air in the bottle. Hot air needs more space than cold air, so the air pressure inside goes up, forcing the water up the straw.

25

Air pressure and flight

Try these experiments to find out how air pressure is used to make an airplane fly.

Hold a sheet of paper by two corners so that one edge touches your bottom lip and the sheet hangs down. Now blow hard over it. What happens?

Now hold two sheets so that they hang down with a small gap between them. What do you expect will happen when you blow into the gap? Try it. Is that what you expected to happen?

You have just shown yourself the principle of flight. What happens is that when air moves at speed, its pressure drops. So when you blow between the pieces of paper, the pressure there is lower than outside. The greater pressure on the outside of the sheets pushes them together. The wings of airplanes are designed in a special way to make use of this principle.

This aircraft wing is folded. The top is rounded and the bottom is flat.

26

Wings

An airplane wing is shaped so that the air on top has to travel farther than the air underneath.

This makes the air on top travel faster, so its pressure drops.

The greater air pressure below lifts the wing, and the airplane. This is how huge modern aircraft stay up in the sky.

The power of pressure

The air around us at sea level presses on everything with a pressure, or force, of about 14.7 pounds on every square inch. Deep in the oceans, thousands of feet down, the pressure of water is enormous. A diver experiences an increase of many pounds per square inch as he or she dives deeper. Submarines are carefully designed so that they are not crushed by the enormous forces.

Left *Water pressure gets higher the deeper you dive. This swimmer has to breathe air that is at higher pressure than normal to keep her lungs working.*

Right *Astronauts no longer need to wear heavy space suits. These astronauts are on board the American Space Shuttle. Inside, scientists have been able to create the right pressure and conditions for humans to live.*

People have learned to live in space too, high above the edge of the *atmosphere*, where there is almost no pressure at all. They have done this by creating an *artificial* atmosphere at normal pressure.

Here on Earth, people have learned to use the power of pressure to make anything from the vacuum cleaner to the hydraulic lift. By understanding its principles, people can use pressure to apply just the right amount of force exactly where they want it.

Glossary

Aerosol A fine mist made of tiny droplets of liquid hanging in the air.

Artificial Made or created by people, rather than existing naturally.

Atmosphere The layer of air that surrounds the earth. It is densest at sea level and becomes thinner the higher you go. In space, there is no air at all.

Balance When two things press against each other with equal force, they are *balanced.*

Ball cock A device—a floating ball connected to a valve—that controls water coming into a toilet cistern.

Blades The flat parts of a propeller that spin around.

Carbon dioxide A colorless gas that is part of the air we breathe.

Cistern The water tank above a toilet. The cistern also contains the flushing mechanism.

Compress To squeeze something together so that it takes up less space than it would normally.

Cylinder A round, hollow tube, such as a length of drainpipe.

Friction The force that makes it hard to push an object across a surface, caused by the two things rubbing against each other.

Hydraulic Something moved or worked by the pressure in a liquid.

Nozzle A small opening with a valve in it at the end of a tube or pipe.

Particles The smallest specks of a substance, often called molecules.

Piston A round plate that fits inside a cylinder and moves up and down in the cylinder.

Pneumatic Something moved or worked by the pressure in air or another gas.

Seal To close tightly so that no air or water can pass through.

Suction The force produced by decreasing the pressure on something so that it takes up more space than it would normally.

Valve A device that controls the flow of a liquid or gas. A valve opens like a door to let the fluid through an opening and closes to stop it.

Books to read

For younger readers:
Air in Action by Robin Kerrod
(Marshall Cavendish, 1990)
Flight by Malcolm Dixon
(Franklin Watts, 1991)
Air & Flight by Barbara Taylor
(Franklin Watts, 1991)

For older readers:
Pressure (Tops Learning, 1978)
The Way Things Work by David
Macaulay (Houghton Mifflin, 1988)
Water at Work by Barbara Taylor
(Franklin Watts, 1991)

Index

Picture acknowledgments

The publishers would like to thank the following for providing the photographs for this book: Cephas Picture Library 12 (Stuart Boreham); NASA/Science Photo Library 29; Sefton Photo Library 26; Tony Stone Worldwide 28 (Chris Harvey); Wayland Picture Library 20; Zefa 4, 8.